MAKING
A NATIVE
PLANT
TERRARIUM

MAKING
A NATIVE
PLANT
TERRARIUM

written and illustrated

by D.J. HERDA

Julian Messner   New York

Manufactured in the United States of America

Design by Philip Jaget

Second Printing, 1979

Library of Congress Cataloging in Publication Data
Herda, D J
    Making a native plant terrarium.

    SUMMARY: Directions for creating and caring for a terrarium, with emphasis on growing
native plants. Lists sources for obtaining native plants by mail.
    1. Glass gardens—Juvenile literature. 2. Wild flower gardening—Juvenile literature. [1.
Terrariums]
I. Title.
SB417.H47   635.9′8   77-10583
ISBN 0-671-32880-8

Contents

To Edwin, Sharmini, Christy, Randy, Shawn, Patty, and David—the best native plant terrarium gardeners I know.

Chapter 1

WHAT'S A TERRARIUM?

Imagine a tiny world, complete with soil, trees, flowers, grass, and rain. It may be the size of a softball, or bigger than a breadbox. But it's alive. And it's a world *you* can make: it's a terrarium.

Terrariums are clear glass or plastic containers that contain an almost complete *ecosystem*, a piece of nature that can function by itself. There are living, growing organisms—the plants. There is soil. There is air. And there is moisture which continually evaporates in the air, condenses back to water, and settles to the ground like rain.

The plants may be arranged with twigs and small stones to look like a woodland scene. Or the soil may slope to resemble hills or mountains with valleys in between. There may be small figurines of animals, or fantastic plastic creatures that look as if they've just stepped off Mars. There may even be live animals like frogs, toads, snakes, and small lizards. (Terrariums with both plants and animals are called *vivariums*.)

There's no end to the different worlds of a terrarium.

This frog lives in a vivarium.

One of the nice things about making a terrarium is that it can be whatever you want it to be. That's one of the reasons terrariums are so popular. There are other reasons, too:

. . . Terrariums are easy to care for. The plants don't need to be *fertilized*, or fed. They don't have to be watered as often as in a flower pot, because terrarium soil stays moist longer.

. . . Terrariums stay beautiful all year long. Since terrariums are kept indoors, you can enjoy growing, blooming plants even during the coldest days of winter.

. . . Perhaps the best reason of all for growing plants in terrariums is that it's fun.

When you select a container, fill it with soil, and tuck in some plants, there's a great thrill in watching the world you made grow bigger and healthier each day.

There are terrariums that cost thousands of dollars and are so valuable they are in museums, along with other great works of art. Some of the best terrariums, though, don't cost thousands of dollars or ten dollars, or even one dollar. They're practically free. These are the native plant terrariums we'll be making.

Native plants are plants that grow naturally where you live. Whether you live in the country or in the heart of the city, there are always plants nearby that would be good in your terrarium.

And once you've planted your first terrarium, you'll find yourself looking forward to making others. Each terrarium you

A very expensive, leaded glass terrarium.

plant will be different from the last, and each will give you joy and a sense of accomplishment.

Chapter 2

HERE A CONTAINER, THERE A CONTAINER

Terrarium containers are everywhere. But to find them, you must use your imagination. Look around the house. Check the kitchen, the basement, the garage. Do you see any clear glass or plastic containers with interesting or unusual shapes?

How about a casserole dish that's no longer used for baking because of a chipped cover? It would make an excellent terrarium for low-growing plants.

Or how about a large pickle jar? It would be fine for taller plants, so long as its mouth is wide enough for your hand to fit through.

Or what about an old glass coffee pot? Wouldn't it make an unusual terrarium? Its shape would make it especially attractive.

But, no matter what container you find around the house, ask someone first if you can use it before turning it into a terrarium!

SOME TYPICAL CONTAINERS

Sometimes, no matter how hard you look, you just won't find a container that would make a good terrarium. In that case, perhaps you can buy one. Discount stores, department stores, dime stores, and supermarkets all have inexpensive containers that would make excellent terrariums.

Or maybe you can ask some of your friends and relatives to keep their eyes open for a container.

Here's a list of some containers that would make good terrariums:

Large glass pitcher
Goldfish bowl (any size)
Aquarium
Large drinking glass
Glass beer stein
Plastic shoe box
Wide-mouth jar
Glass coffee pot

Selecting a Terrarium Container

First, your container should be made of transparent, uncolored glass or plastic so that you can see what's planted inside. After all, part of the fun of having a terrarium is watching the plants grow. Also, if you choose a colored container for your terrarium, your plants won't get all the light they need for proper growth. They'll grow poorly—or not at all.

Secondly, the container should be large enough. Even the smallest plants you find will need two or three inches of growing room and another couple of inches for their roots.

Finally, the mouth (top opening) of the container has to be wide enough for your hand to pass through. How else will you plant and care for your terrarium?

Patty can get her whole forearm into this container, not just her hand!

What Shape Is Best?

Terrarium containers come in all different sizes and shapes. That's what makes them interesting. They're like people. Think of how dull terrariums—or people—would be, if they all looked alike!

Keep alert for a container with an especially unusual shape. Perhaps you'll find a tall glass jar with absolutely straight sides, or one that curves out in the middle like a barrel.

Maybe you'll find a plastic container shaped like a cube, a ball, or even a triangle. It would make a really unusual terrarium!

Whichever you find—whichever you like best—is right for you. No one shape is better than another. But the shape of the container does make a difference in whether or not it will need a cover.

If a container has a wide bottom and narrow opening (just barely wide enough to fit your hand through), it won't need a cover, although you can use one if you like. However, if the mouth is as wide as the bottom, or wider, your container will need a cover. Here's why:

The moisture inside a terrarium is constantly evaporating from the soil. That means it rises up and floats off into the air.

If your container has a wide mouth, a lot of moisture will escape from the container, and the soil will dry out quickly. If the soil gets too dry, the plants inside your terrarium may die.

Most of the moisture evaporates into the air when a wide-mouthed terrarium has no cover.

A cover will keep the moisture in.

If your container has a narrow mouth, or a cover, the moisture will rise up from the soil, strike the sides and top of the container, and *condense*, that is, turn back into droplets of water. These droplets will fall back to the soil. Only a little moisture will escape through the mouth. Therefore, the soil will stay wet longer. And the moisture in the container—

CONDENSATION

humidity—will help keep the plants healthy and strong.

What if you have a container but you can't find a cover for it? You can make just about any size cover you need from plastic wrap. Cover the container with the wrap, fasten it with a rubber band, and trim off the excess with a pair of scissors. If you don't have a rubber band large enough to fit around the top of the container, you can fasten the wrap with clear tape.

Plastic wrap held by a rubber band makes a good terrarium cover.

Glass or Plastic?

Which material is best for a terrarium container—glass or plastic? Each has its good points and bad. A glass container is often less expensive than a clear plastic container of the same size. Glass is more widely available. Also, glass doesn't scratch as easily as plastic.

On the other hand, plastic is lighter in weight and more durable than glass. It won't shatter so easily if dropped.

Glass or plastic—the choice is up to you. Just remember to treat either one carefully and it will be around for years to come.

Chapter 3

SOIL

Soil is the basis for a plant's life. It contains the minerals and salts a plant must have to live.

Plants, like animals, must also have oxygen, which they get from water. It's important that soil be *porous*—loose enough so that water can get through to the roots at the bottom of the container.

When you pick up a handful of garden soil, you have a wonderful collection of sand, clay, weed seeds, small stones, *humus* (twigs, grass, decaying leaves and roots), and many insects, some so small that they can't be seen except through a microscope. The insects help to break down the soil into small *nutrients*, or food, that a plant's roots can draw up and send throughout its system.

That handful of garden soil also has *bacteria*, plants that can only be seen with a microscope, and other organisms in it— some of them harmful to plants.

Buying Soil

Packaged soil you buy in the store is *sterilized*, which means the bacteria have been killed and the soil is disease-free.

Patty looks at all those things in a handful of soil.

If you buy soil for your terrarium, buy an all-purpose potting soil. Along with the soil, you should buy sphagnum moss to add to the soil. The moss will help loosen the soil, making it more porous, while adding some nutrients that will help the plants grow. Mix one handful of moss with each four or five handfuls of soil.

Collecting Soil

If you decide to collect your own soil, you'll have to prepare and sterilize it, but you'll save money.

Collect the soil when the ground is fairly dry. Pick up a handful and examine it. If it's spongy and holds together in a ball when you squeeze it, it's a good, all-purpose soil with plenty of humus in it. If it's hard and rocky, but crumbles under pressure, it hasn't enough humus in it. Add some sphagnum moss or crumbled leaves, grass, or other plant material at a rate of one handful for each three handfuls of soil.

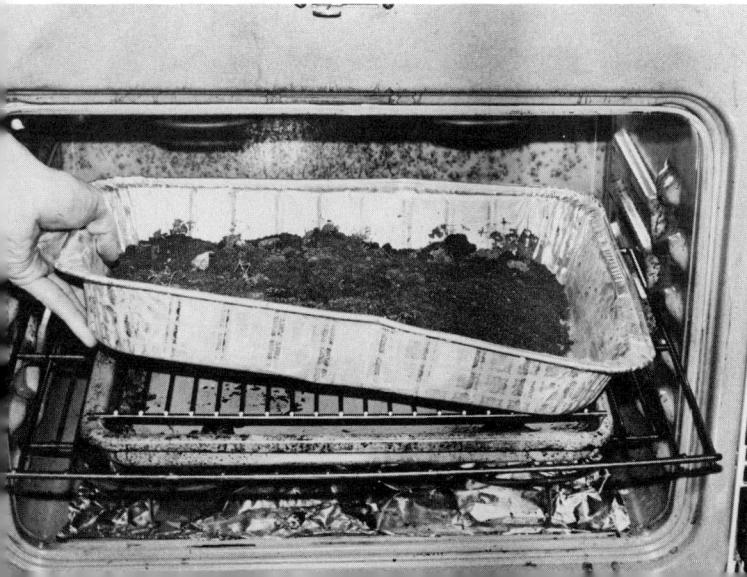

Putting soil in the oven to sterilize it. Remember to use a pot holder when you take the soil container out—or let it cool off in the oven.

After preparing the soil, put the mixture in a big baking dish or pan. Get some help with the oven so you can bake the soil for two hours at 250 degrees F. (121 degrees C.). Then allow the soil to cool before you handle it.

Now your collected soil is sterilized. It has no disease causing organisms in it.

Giving Your Plants the Soil They Need

Store-bought or collected, your all-purpose potting soil may be used as a base for creating other kinds of soils. If you're planting plants that like soil rich in humus, you will need to add one handful of humus to every handful of general potting soil. Humus may be bought in stores, or collected. If collected, humus, like soil, needs to be sterilized.

If you're planting plants that prefer a light, sandy soil, use one handful of general potting soil mix, and add one handful of sand or bird gravel. Make sure the sand is sterilized, if you collect it. The sand or bird gravel will help keep the soil porous (soil has a way of packing down after a while). It will help root-hair growth, which leads to healthy plants. *Root hairs* are tiny, newly-formed roots.

Chapter 4

SUPPLIES FOR YOUR DIGGING EXPEDITION

Once you have your container and soil, you'll need to prepare for collecting and planting your native plants. You'll need to get:

A spade or other digging tool
Gloves
Plastic Bags
Damp paper towels or sheets of newspaper
Note pad
Pencil
Ruler

Spade. If you can find a small spade, good. A collapsible camping spade is good. It opens up to a handle about three feet long, with a blade about eight inches across. It has a sharp point for easy digging in the hardest ground.

If you can't find a spade, you can use a trowel, or even a strong, large spoon. They will work nearly as well, although most hand tools aren't made for hard digging. If you're digging in rocky ground, be careful not to put too much pressure on the tool or it will bend.

Gloves. Sometimes you must dig around in rocky soil to free a plant's roots. Heavy gardener's gloves will protect your hands from scrapes and cuts. But they aren't absolutely necessary.

Plastic Bags. These are an absolute must. Take several with you—one for each plant you plan on digging, and some large ones for soil. Bring some twist ties or pipe cleaners to seal the bags shut.

If you don't place the freshly-dug plants in a sealed plastic bag, the drying effects of the air and wind could damage or even kill the plants.

Damp paper towels or pieces of newspaper to be placed in each plant bag. The damp paper will prevent the delicate roots of the plant from drying out.

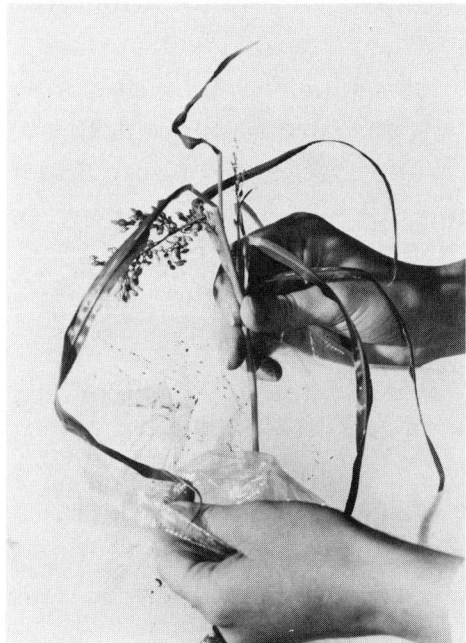

A newly dug native plant being placed in a plastic bag.

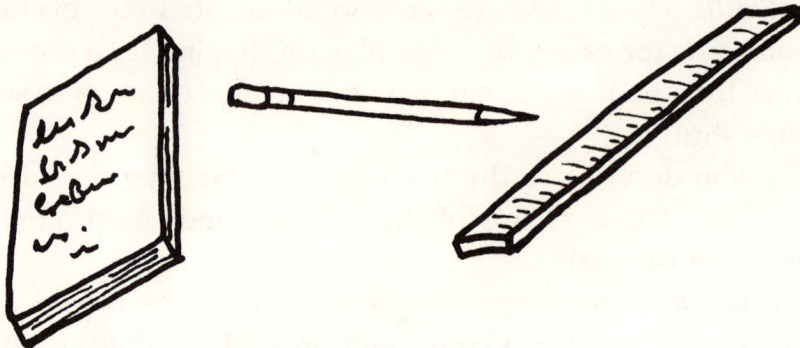

Note pad, pencil, and ruler. Before leaving the house, measure the space in your terrarium from the bottom to the container's top. Then deduct 3 or 4 inches for the depth of the soil. Deduct another inch to allow for growth. The remaining figure tells you the size of the tallest plant you can place in your terrarium. Write that figure down on the note pad so you don't forget it. Then, you can measure each plant you find before digging it up to make sure it's not too tall for the container.

You also need the pad and pencil to make notations in the field. For each plant you dig up, note the kind of soil it's growing in, as well as the plant's living conditions. Is it growing beneath a thich bush where it receives practically no direct sun? Is it growing next to a large rock or mound, where it gets a little sun but spends the rest of the day in shade? Or is it growing in a field where it gets a full day's sun?

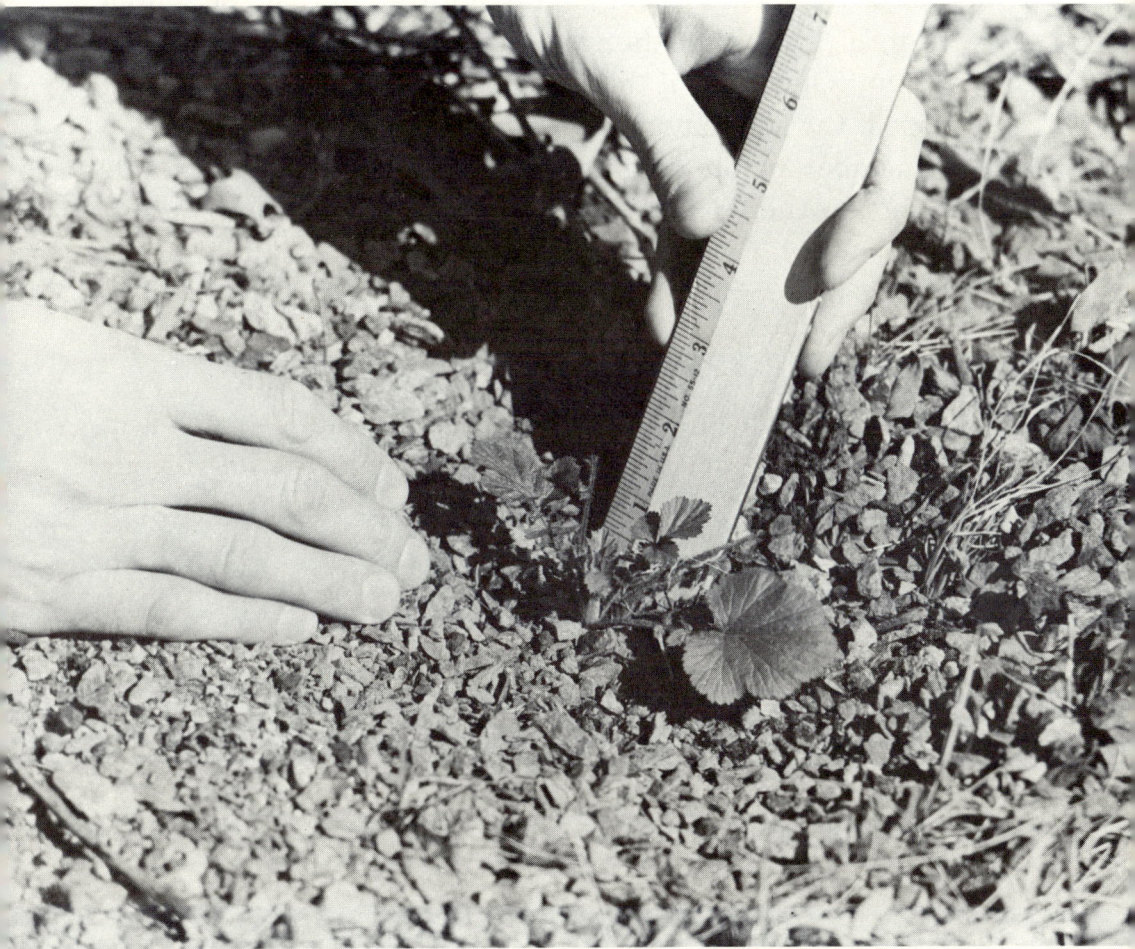

Checking measurements.

33

Make a note, too, about the moisture content of the soil. Pick up a handful and squeeze. Does it feel very moist, a little damp, or dry? If the plant is growing well in that soil, you'll want to give it about the same amount of moisture in your terrarium. Of course, if there have been recent rains or a long dry spell, the soil may not be in its best condition.

Remember, before digging up any plants, that all the plants you choose should need the same amount of sunlight and moisture. Don't mix sun-loving plants with shade-loving plants. It's impossible to meet both these requirements in a single terrarium. And if you place a moisture-loving plant with one that prefers dry soil, one of the plants will suffer.

One area in which you can successfully mix-and-match is in the *kind* of soils you use. By carefully arranging the soil in your terrarium, you can have one plant growing in rich soil next to another growing in sandy soil.

When you've written this information down, place the notepaper in the plastic bag along with the plant. In that way, when you get back inside, the plant and its notes will be to-gether. There'll be no chance for a mixup.

Chapter 5

DIGGING THE PLANTS

When you've found a healthy-looking plant you think will grow well in your terrarium, dig it out of the ground carefully. You want to get as large a root mass with the plant as possible. The more roots that come with the plant, the better its chance for survival. If too many roots are cut off and left behind—or if you accidentally injure a plant—it will go into "shock" and may die.

This native plant came out of the ground with its roots mass in good shape.

Be sure the plants you choose for your terrarium are healthy. Don't worry if a plant has small holes in a couple of its leaves or if a few leaves are cut or brown. This is just a sign of natural wear and tear. All outdoor plants suffer occasional insect attacks. But if the entire plant looks weak, if the leaves have large brown, gray, or yellow splotches all over, beware! That could be a sign of serious trouble—bacteria or fungus attack which will be hard to cure indoors.

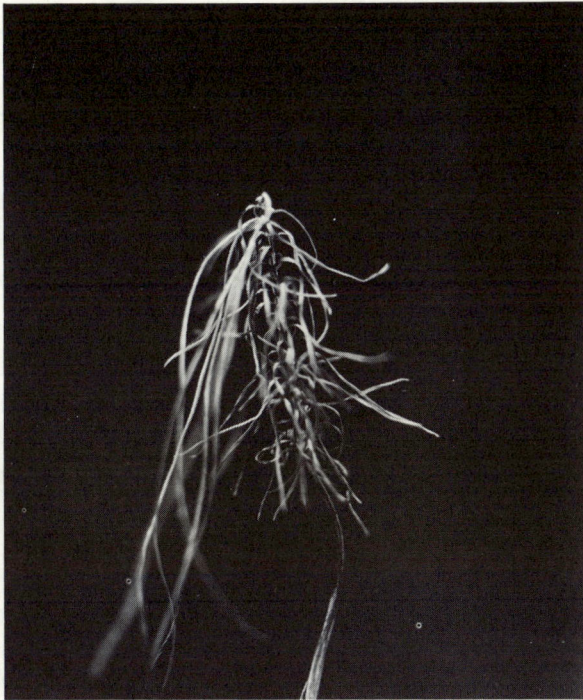

Pine seedling with dried and sagging needles.

Dig only those plants that are growing in a *stand*, or group, of several of the same type. Don't take the last of a *species*, or variety, of plant from one area. You don't want to deprive others of the beauty and enjoyment of seeing a certain type plant simply so you can fill your terrarium. There are plenty of other plants you can select.

The spade is placed some distance away from the plant when digging in so that the roots, spreading underground, will not be cut.

After spading, the plant is removed from the ground by hand, gently.

Chapter 6

YOUR PLANTS COME HOME

After you've dug and bagged the plants you want for your terrarium, bring them into the house. Fill a sink or bucket with cool, but not cold, water. Take one plant from its bag and carefully rinse it off. (Be sure not to lose the notes about the plant's requirements.) Swoosh the plant around to remove all dirt from its roots. Lightly rub the leaves to remove any insects or insect eggs that might be clinging to them.

Examine the roots and leaves of the plant. If there are broken or split roots, *prune*, or cut, them away with scissors. Do the same with the *topgrowth*—the leaves and branches. You can cut back as much as a third of a plant's topgrowth without injuring it. Cut back only as many of the roots as necessary, though. If you cut back too many, the remaining roots won't be able to supply enough food and water to the plant's framework.

After pruning, gently shake the plant to remove excess water, rinse out the plastic bag, and place the plant back inside, along with its note sheet. Do that with each of the plants you've collected, and then line the bags up in your terrarium work area.

Before putting in the soil, wash your container thoroughly in warm water, inside and out, using mild soap and a soft rag or sponge. If the container has tags or labels on it, be sure to remove them now, so they don't show after the terrarium is planted.

If your container is glass, dry with a lint-free cloth, paper towel, or piece of crumpled newspaper. Use only a soft cloth if yours is a plastic container, so you don't scratch it. Make sure you clean off all smudges, and handle the container carefully from this point on. It's much more difficult to clean a container once the soil and plants are inside.

On the very bottom of the container, put a half-inch or more of some type of *drainage material*. Small rocks, pebbles, mar-

Pruning the topgrowth.

bles, charcoal, or gravel at the bottom of the terrarium hold excess moisture from the soil so your plant's roots aren't sitting in an underground puddle. Otherwise, too much water in the soil will force out all the tiny pockets of oxygen which the roots need to breathe. Terrarium soil can be moist, but it should never be saturated, or your plants will drown!

Charcoal is one of the best drainage materials for a terrarium, as it also prevents the soil from becoming too acid, or spoiled. You can buy charcoal chips at pet shops and many department stores.

Place a half-inch layer of drainage material in the bottom of the container. Cover the material with a sheet of cheesecloth, screening, or piece of nylon stocking. That will prevent the soil from washing down into the drainage material and clogging it up.

Place the container on a table or the floor where you're going to work. Place your general potting soil mix nearby, along with a bowl of humus and one of sand. If you can find a soup or gravy ladle, set that out, too. It's an excellent tool for placing soil in the container without smudging the sides.

Adding the Soil

Take a look at the note sheet for one of the plants. If it calls for a light, sandy soil, or a humusy soil, mix it according to the directions on page 28. Then use the ladle, or your hand, to

Randy is preparing to put charcoal into the bottom of his container.

place the soil you need where you want that plant to grow. Put in as much as you think will cover the roots.

Then, using a spoon, or a pencil, dig a hole large enough to hold the plant's roots in the soil. Holding the plant between your thumb and index finger, place the roots in the hole. Gently brush the surrounding soil up against the plant's stem

Shawn is putting sterilized soil into his container. It takes concentration!

with your free fingers. After the roots are completely covered, let go of the plant, and firm the soil down by pressing it with your fingertips. Don't press hard, or you'll damage the roots. Just press hard enough so that the plant stands firm, and all large air pockets beneath the soil are pressed out. Large pockets of air could dry out some of the plant's roots.

Digging a plant hole with a pencil.

Sharmini uses a rubber spatula to help her plant.

Repeat the procedure for the remaining plants in your collection. Of course, if all the plants have the same soil requirements, you can mix up a large batch of the right type soil and cover the bottom of the terrarium with a couple of inches all at once. Then place the plants where you want them one after the other.

Edwin, Christy, and Sharmini are getting ready to plant.

Landscaping

Vary the levels of soil in your terrarium if you have room to do so. Place some plants on high "hills," others in lower "valleys." A landscape in miniature makes a more interesting setting.

You may choose to leave patches of open ground. A bare spot can be every bit as interesting as a plant. It resembles a

A "bank effect"—short plants in front, tall in back or to the side—is good landscaping.

clearing in the woods where you might find rabbits, squirrels, and chipmunks feeding.

After all the plants are in, you can add some attractive stones to resemble boulders—or a few small twigs to look like fallen logs or dead trees. Brush a little of the soil up against them. That way, they'll look natural, as though they've been there for years.

Brushing up the soil to make sure the plant is sitting firmly.

Making the Terrarium
Your Own World

What else can you add to your terrarium to give it your own, personal touch? How about some tiny woodland figures, like rabbits, raccoons, and squirrels? Or maybe some plastic dinosaurs set among your plants to resemble a prehistoric

forest? Small cows, horses, and ducks turn terrariums into miniature farmlands.

Would you like a lake in your terrarium? You can make one by placing a small pocket mirror on the ground and covering the edges with pebbles or soil. Then place a small boat or a bunch of swimming ducks in the center of the lake. The reflections in the "water" will be an attractive addition to the terrarium.

These shell turtles please their terrarium owner.

Final Clean-Up

Once you've finished decorating your terrarium, it's time for watering and a final clean-up. If the soil is already moist, you can skip the watering. If it's dry, take a spray bottle filled with cool water and gently spray the plants, washing off any dirt that may have stuck to the leaves. If you don't have a spray bottle, you can dip your fist in a bucket of water and shake the drops onto your plants.

But don't overdo it! You want the soil to be moist, not soggy.

Finally, take a damp paper towel, or soft cloth, and wipe the inside walls of the terrarium to remove excess moisture and any remaining dirt. If the container has a cover, put it on.

Then step back and admire!

Chapter 7

CARING FOR YOUR TERRARIUM

If some of your plants seem to wilt at first, don't worry. All plants suffer transplanting shock. After they adjust to their new surroundings, they should begin to perk up.

Terrariums don't require much care, but you should know a couple of things they'll need to stay healthy.

Light

You can meet the plants' light needs by placing your planted terrarium well back from a window (full shade), nearer the window for a couple of hours of light daily (partial shade), or on the window sill where they receive a full day of direct sun (full sun).

Avoid placing your new terrarium in direct sunlight for a few days after planting. Even those that need good light should receive only partial light until they've adjusted to their new growing conditions and whatever pruning they've undergone.

After a few days, you can move your terrarium to a well-lit shelf or table near an east- or north-facing window. The sun at either of these windows won't be so strong that it "cooks" the plants. Yet it will supply all the rays the plants need to produce food for healthy growth.

In winter months, you can keep your terrarium in front of a

south or west window, if you desire. But avoid these two exposures during the hottest days of summer or the intense heat will certainly damage or destroy the plants.

Moisture

You'll want to adjust the amount of light and moisture according to the notes you took when collecting the plants. Moisture-loving plants will need a damper soil than those plants that grow best in dry, sandy soil.

A terrarium is "in balance" if it has just the right amount of moisture for the number of plants growing inside it.

Most terrarium plants die because of too *much* moisture in the container, not too little. Remember that a terrarium holds moisture for long periods of time. If beads of water form on the sides of the terrarium and cause the glass to look foggy, the soil is too moist. Remove the cover for a day or two to allow some of the moisture to escape. If it's an uncovered terrarium, the extra moisture should clear by itself within a day or two.

Watering

If you think your terrarium needs watering, use the "touch test" to be sure. Stick your finger into the soil up to the first knuckle. Then pull your finger out and examine the soil that clings to it. If the soil is dry, it needs more water. Remember to stick your finger down into the soil, not just on top. You want to find out if the soil at the plants' roots is damp or dry.

Whenever you water your terrarium plants, it's important not to use water right from the faucet. Most tap water is treated with such chemicals as fluorine and chlorine. While these chemicals may be beneficial to human beings, they're not very healthful for plants.

The "touch test."

In order to eliminate these chemicals from tap water, fill a container with water and allow it to stand overnight. The chemicals will *oxidize*, or change into harmless elements. Then the water is safe for your plants.

Pruning

After a couple of weeks of caring for your terrarium, you'll notice the plants starting to grow. Some grow faster than others. Sooner or later, many plants threaten to outgrow their homes.

You can prevent this from happening by pruning. Just take a small pair of scissors and snip the tall plants back. Don't cut more than a third off their original height. Make the cuts just above a leaf or branch. The plants will soon heal their wounds and start growing once again. Often they grow out instead of up. You'll have fuller, bushier plants that don't outgrow the container so fast.

So Sad

Occasionally, despite all your best efforts, you'll notice one of your plants starting to droop. Day by day, it will get weaker and paler, until finally it dies.

Don't let the loss of a plant or two discourage you. All plants die eventually. Some live only a year. Others may not adapt to the type of soil, humidity, and light conditions in your terrarium.

If you find that one plant won't grow for you, replace it with a different type. Sooner or later, you'll have a terrarium filled with plants that grow well together.

Beating the Bugs

If you sterilize your soil and drainage material, and wash all collected plants carefully before planting them, you should have no problem with insects—those gnawing, flying, or tunneling little creatures that can turn a beautiful healthy plant into a wilted mess.

But, occasionally, either insects or their eggs may get past you and into your terrarium. If that happens, you're in for trouble!

Outdoors, insects have plenty of natural predators that feed on them and help hold them in check—birds, snakes, frogs, toads, newts, and other insects. But in the protected surroundings of a terrarium, they can multiply fast and really do some harm.

If you detect insect damage on your plants, take an infested leaf to your nearest garden center or plant store and ask for help. A trained person should be able to tell you which insect is to blame and what to do to get rid of it.

If an insecticide is recommended, ask your parents to apply it, as most insecticides are dangerous. Never handle insecticides or their containers except under close supervision of an adult.

If you treat the plants carefully, you'll be amazed at how long most will live. Like human beings, they're constantly growing, constantly changing. And that is part of the challenge and fun of owning a terrarium.

LISTING OF NATIVE PLANTS FOR THE TERRARIUM

The following native plants do well in terrariums when their growing requirements are met. They can be found in fields, roadsides, and vacant lots.

Heights listed are maximum heights, in the wild. Remember that you can train most plants shorter by pruning their tips.

Before digging any native plants, be sure you choose ones with about the same light and moisture requirements.

You can check with the Department of Natural Resources in your state for other local plants—and for those plants you may not pick.

American Brooklime, Speedwell
Height: 6 to 15 inches.
Bloom: Bright blue in summer.
Soil: General.
Range: Throughout U.S.

Bearberry
Height: 6 inches.
Bloom: White pink-tipped flowers in spring.
Soil: Sandy.
Range: Eastern U.S., Yellowstone Park, Montana, Northwestern U.S., California.

Bladder-Campion, White Vein
Height: 6 to 24 inches.
Bloom: White to pinkish in summer.
Soil: Sandy.
Range: Northern U.S.

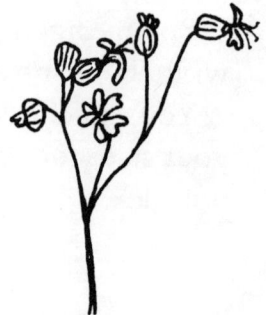

Buckbean, Bogbean, Marsh Trefoil
Height: 10 inches.
Bloom: White in early summer.
Soil: Rich humus.
Range: Northern U.S.

Bunchberry, Crackerberry
Height: 10 inches
Bloom: White in spring and summer.
Soil: Rich humus.
Range: South to West Virginia.

Climbing Wild Cucumber
Height: a vine reaching 20 feet.
Bloom: Greenish-white in summer.
Soil: Rich humus.
Range: West to Idaho.

Crested Dwarf Iris
Height: 4 inches.
Bloom: Lavender-blue in spring.
Soil: Rich humus with plenty of sand.
Range: Maryland to Georgia and west to Oklahoma.

Dandelion
Height: 3 to 14 inches.
Bloom: Yellow in spring and summer.
Soil: General.
Range: Throughout U.S.

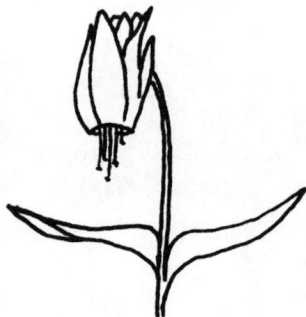

Dog's-Tooth Violet
Height: 12 to 20 inches.
Bloom: White to yellowish in early spring.
Soil: Rich humus.
Range: Throughout U.S.

Field Chickweed
Height: 10 inches.
Bloom: White in early summer.
Soil: General.
Range: Northern U.S.

Forget-Me-Not
Height: 15 inches.
Bloom: Light blue in spring, summer, fall.
Soil: Rich humus, with plenty of moss kept moist.
Range: South to North Carolina.

Goldthread
Height: 6 inches.
Bloom: White in early summer.
Soil: Rich humus.
Range: Northern U.S. and in Appalachians of Tennessee.

Hepatica, Liverleaf
Height: 5 inches.
Bloom: Lilac, blue, white, or pink in early spring.
Soil: General.
Range: South to Florida.

Indian Pipe, Pinesap
Height: 9 inches.
Bloom: White in summer, northern states; November to December, southern states.
Soil: Rich humus.
Range: Throughout U.S.
Comments: Avoid direct sun!

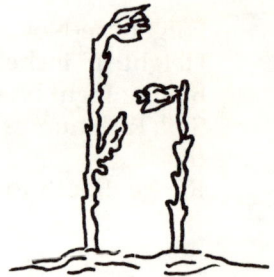

Lichens
Height: 2 inches.
Bloom: None.
Soil: General to slightly humusy and kept moist.
Range: Throughout U.S.
Comments: Lichens are not one plant but two. They are green algae surrounded by a colorless fungi (both are tiny plants). Lichens make an excellent addition to most terrariums.

Maidenhair Spleenwort
Height: 6 inches.
Bloom: None.
Soil: General, with powdered lime added.
Range: Eastern U.S. and Alaska.
Comments: Avoid direct sun!

Maiden Pink
Height: 6 to 12 inches.
Bloom: Brilliant pink in May and June.
Soil: General to lightly sandy.
Range: Throughout U.S.

Morning-Glory
Height: a vine.
Bloom: White or cream-colored in March
through May.
Soil: Rich humus.
Range: Throughout U.S.

Oxeye Daisy, Common White Daisy
Height: 15 to 24 inches.
Bloom: White with yellow center in summer.
Soil: General.
Range: Throughout U.S.

Pasqueflower
Height: 6 to 14 inches.
Bloom: Violet in early spring.
Soil: Light with plenty of drainage material; sandy.
Range: Illinois north and west to Colorado and in Alaska.

Rattlebox
Height: 4 to 12 inches.
Bloom: Yellow in summer.
Soil: Sandy.
Range: South from South Dakota.

Red Clover
Height: 8 to 24 inches.
Bloom: Magenta or pink in early spring.
Soil: Sandy.
Range: Throughout U.S.

Round-Leaved Sundew
Height: 9 inches.
Bloom: White in summer.
Soil: Humus-enriched sphagnum moss kept moist.
Range: Northern U.S.

Rusty Woodsia
Height: 6 inches.
Bloom: None.
Soil: General to slightly humusy.
Range: Northeastern U.S.
Comments: Avoid direct sun!

Self-Heal, Heal-All
Height: 6 to 13 inches.
Bloom: Purple in spring and summer.
Soil: General to lightly sandy.
Range: Throughout U.S.

Sweet White Violet
Height: 5 inches.
Bloom: White with purple in early spring.
Soil: General.
Range: South to Georgia and Louisiana.

Wild Lily-of-the-Valley
Height: 6 inches.
Bloom: White in spring.
Soil: Rich humus.
Range: South to North Carolina and west to South Dakota.
Comments: POISONOUS! Do not take plant or water in which it may have been into mouth.

Wild Mint
Height: 12 to 22 inches.
Bloom: White or lavender in summer and fall.
Soil: General.
Range: South to Georgia; west to Nebraska; also in far west.

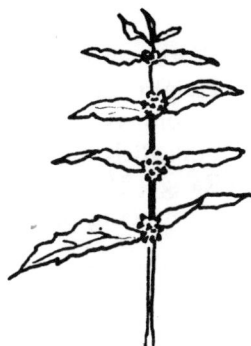

Wild Onion
Height: 10 to 16 inches.
Bloom: White, pink, or rose-colored in summer.
Soil: Sandy.
Range: Throughout U.S.

Wintergreen, Checkerberry, Teaberry
Height: 5 inches.
Bloom: White or pinkish in late spring and summer.
Soil: Rich humus.
Range: South to Georgia.

Wood Anemone, Windflower
Height: 12 inches.
Bloom: White with gold in spring.
Soil: Rich humus.
Range: Throughout U.S., with the western
form being pale pink or pale blue.

Starting with Seeds

Along with collecting native plants, you might consider collecting and planting the seeds from several native and commonly available plants. Most seeds *germinate*, or sprout, well in the high humidity of a terrarium, and many seedlings grow exceptionally fast and hardy. Keep the soil moist until the seeds have sprouted.

While not all fruit and vegetables grow well in a terrarium due to the high humidity or the shallow root space available, some grow surprisingly well. These are easy to grow and are easy to buy in the market:

Grapefruit/Kumquat/Lemon
Lime/Orange/Tangerine

These trees are all members of the *citrus* group. They range over the southern U.S. Their fruits, which are easily bought, contain the seeds, or pits. These may be removed, washed, dried, and planted in a rich, humusy soil. As the seeds sprout, the *seedlings*, or young plants, should be given good indirect light for best growth. When the plants outgrow the terrarium, they can be transplanted to pots and grown as attractive houseplants.

Dates
Height: 10 feet.
Bloom: None.
Soil: Sandy.

Unpasteurized date pits, available from many health food stores, are the only ones that will sprout. Plant several horizontally, about one inch deep. Transplant to larger pots when plants outgrow the container.

Avocado
Height: 30 feet.
Bloom: None.
Soil: Rich and humusy.

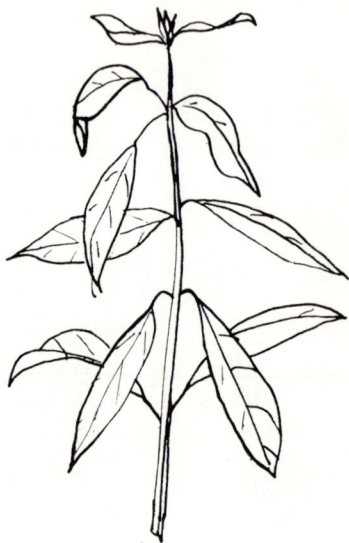

Select a soft, ripe avocado and remove the pit without damaging it. Plant the pit, broad or thick end down, with about one-quarter protruding from the soil. After the plant has at least two sets of leaves, you may prune back additional growth from the tip to form a bushier, fuller plant.

Black Pine/Jack Pine
Red Pine/White Pine

There are many species of native American pine trees suitable for growing in a terrarium while young. Pines are slow growers, requiring humid conditions and rich, humusy soil. As the pines outgrow the terrarium, they should be transplanted to a pot or in the ground. Seeds may be purchased through the mail, or the cones may be collected in winter. Soak the unopened cones in a tub of warm water for 30 minutes to an hour, then remove them and allow to dry. As the cones open, the seeds can be shaken free. These seeds may then be planted. Several black pine tree seeds I collected in this manner were planted in a terrarium and have grown three inches in one year.

Starting with Plant Tops

Carrot
Height: 8 inches.
Bloom: None.
Soil: Sandy.

Cut one-half inch off the top of a carrot and sink it in the soil. Keep the soil moist—but not drenched—and place container in direct light. After a while, the green growth will die back.

85

Pineapple
Height: 3 feet.
Bloom: None.
Soil: Sandy.

Cut the top off a fully ripened, soft pineapple, leaving about one inch of fruit beneath. Pull off the lower few leaves and allow to dry overnight. Bury the fruit base in soil, tamp down firmly, and keep soil moist until new foliage appears at top. As lower leaves turn yellow, they may be removed.

Native Plants by Mail

If you live in an area where native plants aren't widely available, you may want to purchase plants or seeds from one of the sources listed below. Before ordering, send for a catalog and current price list.

Garden Place (Catalog 50¢)
6780 Heisley Road
Mentor, OH 44060

Bluestone
3200 Jackson Street
Mentor, OH 44060

Green Horizons
500 Thompson
Kerrville, TX 78028

Conley's Garden Center (Catalog 35¢)
Boothbay Harbor, ME 04538

Mincemoyer Nurseries (Catalog 25¢)
Rt. 526
Jackson, NJ 08527

Woodstream Nursery (Catalog 15¢)
P.O. Box 510
Jackson, NJ 08527

Clyde Robin (Catalog $1.00)
P.O. Box 2855
Castro Valley, CA 94546

Griffey's Nursery
Rt. 3, Box 17A
Marshall, NC 28753

INDEX

touch test, 60
trees, 9, 51
trowel, 30
twigs, 25, 51

V

vivariums, 10

W

water, 25, 41, 53
watering, 9, 12, 53, 54, 60
weeds, 25
wilt, 56
wind, 31
worlds, 10, 12, 52

ABOUT THE AUTHOR

D. J. HERDA was educated at DePaul University, Roosevelt University, and Columbia College, and received a B.A. in creative writing and journalism. He became a reporter for the *Economist* newspapers, Chicago, and articles editor of *The Elks Magazine,* and taught music theory and composition and fiction writing before going free-lance. Mr. Herda has written a number of books and plays for both adults and young people, and is a book reviewer for *The American West*. He lives in Madison, Wisconsin.

5346

635.9 Herda, D. J.
HER
    Making a native
      plant terrarium

DATE			